# Best Places to Retire: The Top 10 Most Affordable Waterfront Places for Retirement

By: Clayton Geoffreys

# Table of Contents

# Foreword

One of the most important things to consider when planning your retirement is where to live. Finding affordable towns to live in can be a challenge in today's day and age. It's important you stay as much within the 4% rule as possible (which states that if you withdraw at a rate of four percent of your retirement portfolio, you can sustain your current lifestyle while accounting for inflation). Aside from considering affordability, you also need to consider the overall quality of life that you'll experience living in that particular town. For example, it's important to retire in a town where there are readily accessible health care centers as well as reasonable commutes to community events. Hopefully from reading *Best Places to Retire: The Top 10 Most Affordable Waterfront Places for Retirement,* I can provide you with a basic understanding of a few perfect towns to consider for retiring on a budget. Thank you for purchasing my book. Hope you enjoy and if you do, please do not forget to leave a review! Also, check out my website at claytongeoffreys.com to join my exclusive list where I let you know about my latest books. To thank you for your purchase, you can go to my site to download a free copy of _33 Life Lessons: Success Principles, Career Advice & Habits of Successful People_. In the book, you'll learn from some of the greatest thought leaders of different industries on what it takes to become successful and how to live a great life.

Cheers,

_Clayton Geoffreys_

# Introduction

Retirement is one of the biggest goals in a person's life. Thus, there are several things to consider in determining where the best place is to settle during retirement. While a lot of thought goes into the how and when, you want to make sure that you are getting the dream retirement setting you want because you work so hard for it.

One of the biggest dreams for a retirement setting is somewhere near the water, but even that depends on the preferences of the retirees about what they would want to see in a waterfront property. Just like buying a home that is perfect for your situation, selecting a waterfront property is not like most homes in suburban cul de sacs, nor is it like country living.

Waterfront locations can be more than just the typical beach setting along the Pacific Ocean, such as California; or near the Gulf of Mexico and/or the

Atlantic Ocean, as in areas like Texas, Florida, and the Carolinas. There are also tropical islands with sandy beaches that are separate from mainland countries, which could be extremely expensive – these include Hawaii, Cuba, and Belize.

In addition to living along a beach, there are plenty of lakes and rivers surrounded by beautiful forests that can be paradise for an outdoor-person. A home where you are just seconds away from a private dock next to your backyard where you can do some fishing. Some homes are built right up against the lake where you can actually fish from your deck.

Purchasing a waterfront property is a rather unique investment. Therefore, there are a lot of factors to consider when it comes to purchasing a waterfront home:

## Determining What You Need

One of the most critical steps potential buyers should take in their search for a future waterfront home is to determine their intended use for the property. Potential buyers should think about what they would use it for and determine if their prospective waterfront property is a good fit for their needs. One question they could ask themselves would be, "Do I want to do fishing or am I mostly looking for a good view?"

These types of questions will help determine the difference between having a beach and having a deck right up against the body of water. Ask the real estate agent as many questions as possible to develop a better understanding of what you could expect from the property.

## Activities

Another big factor in selecting your waterfront home is the available outdoor activities that you might enjoy doing. You need to have something fun to do out there, especially if your property is in a secluded part of the country.

For example, those who enjoy going out on boats must consider the size of their ship during the property search because many waterfront homes aren't designed to have a large boat parked behind it. There's also a concern with the property not being able to host a larger vessel because of the depth of the water. Oyster beds and tides are other things that also need to be considered.

While there are those who prefer wide open waters for boating, some prospective buyers would prefer to experience the water using a canoe or a kayak. These people prefer a much closer way to commune with the surrounding nature, which is enjoyed more in a smaller and quieter lake without jet skiers flying around behind speedboats.

When it comes to prospective homeowners who enjoy fishing, there are waterfront options where there is easy access to the neighboring body of water. But if you hope to catch a large variety of fish on your line, you'll want to consider having a home that is next to a deeper body of water that can host different breeds – like cold water types.

## Lifestyle Requirements

In addition to making sure you can enjoy certain hobbies, your perfect waterfront home should also meet additional lifestyle needs that you may have. In the event that you would need medical attention, you would want to make sure that the property is within close proximity to a medical center – especially if you're retiring at an advanced age and if medical conditions, such as heart disease, runs in your family.

If you frequently travel for business, you may want a property that doesn't require more than an hour's drive to the nearest airport. Finally, there might be family members who prefer a lake while others might prefer the ocean. A compromise you might make would be to purchase a lakefront property that is just a short drive away from the ocean. This arrangement will give everyone the chance to enjoy the best of both worlds and satisfy both preferences.

## Perform a Scouting Report on Properties

There are a lot of things to consider when it comes to looking for a waterfront property. These usually include many of the same parameters used when looking for any other type of real estate to purchase. The first thing to keep in mind is the old adage of "location, location, location" – this means making rounds to different areas of the country to see what type of waterfront property feels right to you.

When looking at different properties within your budget, there are a lot of factors to keep in mind that goes beyond just the home that you will be living in – which is why real estate agents market these homes as waterfront "properties." You're also paying more money for the land that comes with where your bed rests.

Various waterfront properties, such as those along rivers, lakes, and ocean beaches are not exactly the same. Each type of property offers different advantages and disadvantages for the prospective buyer. Many real estate agents will go over various points of consideration that are important when looking for a waterfront property:

- *Beaches* – Having a sandy shore can provide an extremely pleasant experience that can be enjoyed by everyone in the family, including younger grandchildren who want to play during the warmer months in the summer.
- *View* – Those who are more advanced in age won't be as active on the beachfront. This means that their priority might be having a beautiful view from the deck with their favorite outdoor

seating to see the sights of nature with a good beverage and a chance to enjoy some peace and quiet.

- *An even, level lot* – Many prospective owners prefer to have a level lot that is flat, and sometimes tough, because many waterfront properties often have a steep decline from the grade of the land, which can be difficult for many elderly owners who might find going down to the beach a difficult and unpleasant task.

- *Proximity to the water* – Many waterfront properties are starting to be built within 100 feet from the lake, river or ocean. Having homes within that proximity provides an up-close and personal look at the wildlife that surrounds your waterfront property. Another benefit from being close to the water is being able to keep an eye on the younger ones at play.

- *Privacy* – A big reason why many prospective buyers are interested in a waterfront property is primarily the chance to gain some privacy, avoiding the typical hustle and bustle of the larger cities. While there are some properties that only allow about 50 feet of space between you and the next home, many are hoping for at least 150 to 200 feet of distance for a better sense of privacy.

If a waterfront property scores a perfect score in the above-mentioned qualities, it is likely to be worth millions. This means that only a very small percentage of retirees could afford it, even with years of saving into a retirement fund. Depending on the area your potential waterfront property resides in, there are other things that have to be taken into consideration.

Some of the challenges associated with waterfront properties would likely be larger bills, such as utilities, and other costs that cover the roads leading to your waterfront property and – in some cases – the need for a functional septic system. These are items that are usually readily available in normal properties and homes but are not always guaranteed amenities when it comes to waterfront properties – especially in more secluded areas.

It would be major advantage for prospective owners if a property next to larger bodies of water already has an existing seawall or dock because obtaining the proper permits to build these structures can be an extremely challenging task. These are just some of the challenges that need to be considered in buying a waterfront property. That is why it is highly suggested to hire a specialized real estate agent who will guide you through the complexity associated with buying a waterfront property.

# Great Waterfront Places to Retire In

## 1. Myrtle Beach, South Carolina

### Why is it a Great Place to Retire?

One of the perks about retiring in Myrtle Beach is that the state of South Carolina doesn't put a tax on Social Security benefits. The State also helps retirees receive a generous retirement-income deduction when it comes time to calculate state income tax for the fiscal year. Tax rates are generally lower than the national average between four and six percent of a home's market value.

The coastal city along the Atlantic Ocean has a population of just above 27,000 residents. This is despite its popularity as one the best places to visit in the United States of America – with an estimated number of 14 million visitors who arrive in the area every year. While the city only has 27,000 residents, the entire metropolitan area – which includes much of

Horry County and Georgetown County in South Carolina and part of Brunswick County in North Carolina – has a population of more than 465,000 people.

## Local Community

Because of the large number of tourists, most of the city's economy comes from a large number of hotels, resorts, and other attractions that are continuously developed, which range from entertainment, retail sales, and places to eat. While many people shy away from large tourist towns, there are plenty of things to enjoy as a potential permanent resident of Myrtle Beach.

When it comes to the rates of utilities and other living expenses, Myrtle Beach has prided itself as one of the most cost-effective places to live in the United States – but that doesn't mean there isn't a lot to do in the area.

For starters, Myrtle Beach is definitely a golfer's paradise with more than 100 different golf courses. With this plenty of golf courses, there is at least one golf course that fits everyone's abilities – ranging from Par-3 courses to those frequented by professional players in the Professional Golf Association (PGA) and other high-level tournaments. One of the top-rated courses in this area is the Dunes Golf and Beach Club – which features one of Golf Insider magazine's Top 25 courses with a rating of 8.8 out of 10.

This course, along with Calendonia, True Blue, and the TPC of Myrtle Beach can easily cost about $100 per player to golf a round of 18 holes – but each course offers a beautiful environment of trees, ocean, sand, and other parts of nature. Being able to play a round at every golf course in Myrtle Beach would be a perfect way to spend retirement for some people – especially if you are able to golf a unique course every day, which will definitely prevent boredom.

Millions of rounds of golf have been played through all 120 golf courses, including a record number of 4.2 million in 2007 alone. The most popular golf courses include Arcadian Shores Golf Club, Myrtle Beach National Golf Course, Whispering Pines Golf Course and Palmetto Greens.

The prices of waterfront properties and other real estate are generally low when compared to the rest of the country. This might be one of the biggest factors why it might be great to choose this area as your retirement setting. According to Zillow.com, the average single family home costs about $297,000 – this is less compared to above $300,000 in 2014. The site also reported that many homes are almost half the price in North Myrtle Beach – a resort town that was created in 1967 from four existing municipalities in Myrtle Beach.

Even if you can't buy property, there are many rental agents who can help you enjoy some additional beachfront relaxation without having to deal with the larger populations of nearby metropolitan cities.

One of the most unique attractions of Myrtle Beach is the "Grand Strand," which is the affectionate nickname for the stretch of uninterrupted beach that goes from Little River to Georgetown. Myrtle Beach is included in that stretch of a little more than 60 miles in total. Myrtle Beach features a boardwalk that is considered the third best in the United States by *National Geographic* magazine.

Another part of the Myrtle Beach region to enjoy is Pawley's Island – a small town in nearby Georgetown County and about 25 miles south of Myrtle Beach. The history of this waterfront beach area dates back to the early American settlements from the 1700s. It has since then become a beautiful community where people can walk the beaches barefoot and enjoy a laid-back lifestyle.

The activities in the area include searching for fresh crabs in adjacent creeks, fishing, and setting up a rope hammock, waiting for a gentle breeze to rock you to sleep while looking at a beautiful view of the Atlantic Ocean. The town website prides itself in the conservation of an unaffected and casual stretch of beach that features additional sand dunes.

In addition to all of the above mentioned perks of retiring in Myrtle Beach, folks can also enjoy more of an active lifestyle - thanks not only to the earlier mentioned golf courses, but also to having a community that features various art groups, community service organizations, religious groups, medical facilities, and other professional associations that offer multiple opportunities to be involved and help others through various volunteer activities.

Additionally, Myrtle Beach is also known for having one of the country's best healthcare systems to support the growing retirement population that have moved into its shores. The city's doctors and health care professionals have received various award-winning honors through the multiple centers.

Overall, the area is a comfortable place to live in when it comes to the year-round weather. The summer will provide the most heat with temperatures falling between the low 80s and low 90s during the day, and somewhere near 70 degrees at night. The winters are mild and short with temperatures falling to highs between 57 and 61 degrees, with the nights a lot colder in the mid-to-upper 30s.

Snow is very rare in Myrtle Beach, like most of the Atlantic Coast region. Thus, if you hate the winters experienced in the Midwest and the Northeast, then a place like Myrtle Beach will likely be one of the best options to consider for your retirement.

## 2. Boynton Beach, Florida

### Why is it a Great Place to Retire?

While Florida has plenty of options for places to enjoy the waters of the Atlantic Ocean and the Gulf of Mexico, Boynton Beach stands out among the extremely busy strips between Miami and West Palm Beach. These areas have extremely large amounts of population because of the attraction of living along those white sandy beaches and having the constant sun welcome you as you sit or stand outside on your home's porch. The climate here is consistently warm with the nearby water ready to cool you off in case the temperature rises too high on some occasion.

This is the reason why the state of Florida is considered by many experts as one of the places that have the most number of retirees among each of the United States. With the combination of the amount of people wanting to move to Florida and the benefits of the warm climate, the cost of living is much greater –

requiring a very strong retirement portfolio to help secure a new home. The least expensive options are within the inland section of the state located in the northern half of the state.

But the people who live in cities, such as Naples, will find that real estate prices are higher due to the climate and interest, as well as the number of ocean-related activities that are available in some of these areas, such as surfing, boating, fishing, scuba diving, and water skiing. These activities are enjoyed twice as much because of the double coastlines -- thanks to the waters of the Atlantic Ocean on the eastern side of Florida, and the Gulf of Mexico on the western side

The only other state that might be able to rival the popularity of Florida is California, which has several more miles of coastline that faces the waters of the Pacific Ocean. This means there are several more cities, towns, and communities that can offer a unique variety of activities to enjoy and sights to see, depending on the location of the property – be it the north, central, or south portion of California.

However, Florida has a much more consistent climate that features warm weather. What Florida offers is a diverse collection of cultures that not only features the influence of Mexico, but also the culture of some of the South American countries. There are also multiple Caribbean nations like Cuba and Puerto Rico. Having these various influences help create a chance for American citizens in Florida to experience a wide variety of restaurant cuisine, theater groups, and other retail businesses that give Florida a diverse environment to live in.

Among the most popular options are Miami and Palm Beach – two of the top choices among people who want to live in the state of Florida. However, those who don't have millions in their retirement fund may opt to find other locations that might have lower costs of living while still offering a close proximity to the waters.

Boynton Beach is in the middle of two highly populated areas in the Southeast. It continues to offer a small-town atmosphere for retirees who love the concept of the classic architectural charm that Florida has been known for.

The cost of living does vary, depending on the size of home you want to have and how close to the water you would like to be. For example, Zillow.com lists a waterfront home with three bedrooms for $1.2 million, while another on the city's Ocean Boulevard is listed at nearly $4 million. However, other listings closer to the mainland can be purchased for a fraction of the cost. You might not be right next to the water – but the beaches are just a short drive away.

If you don't feel like buying a property for millions of dollars, there are apartments that are both near to the coast and the town that are not as expensive if you have a steady monthly income from your retirement portfolio. Imagine being able to live comfortably with two bedrooms and one bath near the water for only $1,050 per month – according to some listings on Realtor.com. However, larger homes will include a much larger price tag, with prices hovering closer to the $5,000 per month rate as you move closer to the coast.

Among the reasons why people like to move to Boynton Beach is the beautiful white-sand beaches that go up and down the coast, which is accessible through three municipal parks. Despite the higher cost of living as compared to other places, this suburban coastal city offers a very casual and down to earth atmosphere among the residents. The chances of approaching someone who will act snooty or snobby to each other are a lot lower than in other high-priced neighborhoods.

One of the biggest factors to consider is the climate that one can expect in their future retirement home in Florida. In the winter, it won't get too cold from Jack Frost nipping at your toes. The average temperature in January stays at around 60 degrees. In the summer months, while there are some hot days, the peak-highs usually remain in the lower 80s in June and July.

One concern with living on the Florida Coast is the risk of hurricanes, which bring damaging winds, rains, and tidal waves that can destroy homes and entire neighborhoods. If you are going to live in Boynton Beach, or any other coastal part of Florida, you need to be aware of evacuation routes, emergency services, and have a very good insurance plan to be adequately prepared – which will also cost a very pretty penny.

**Local Community**

For the retiree who enjoys the outdoors, there are a number of options to enjoy the outside views of Boynton Beach. Golf enthusiasts can play a round of nine or 18 holes at The Links at Boynton Beach, It offers an 18-hole par-71 course that is at-par with PGA standards, as well as a 9-hole executive length course that offers five different tee sets for all family members and their respective skill levels.

There are also several city-owned parks and recreation centers that offer something for just about every active lifestyle – including fishing from the Atlantic Coast, joining a boating club, tennis, snorkeling, scuba diving, surfing, and paddle-boarding. Many of the parks are right next to the water as well, including Harvey E. Oyer, Jr. Park with a boat launch into the nearby ocean.

Additionally, the city's Art Center provides various classes for adults who want to learn some new hobbies like painting, sculpting, and other fine arts. Classes for the said activities usually run up to three days a week. The nearby civic center and the Hester Center also provide residents and tourists with several programs and other forms of entertainment in theater, comedy, and music that are suitable for children to adults – most of which you can credit to the Boynton Beach Arts Commission.

The tourists might be one of the disadvantages you could expect from making Boynton, or any place in Florida, a home during your retirement. In fact, Boynton Beach's local economy is very much dependent on the tourism market. This is also true with the thriving retail options. The other big ticket factor is real estate after those tourists come down to visit. They love the area and have the same goal as you do – moving down there after they retire.

Because of that influx of interested people, there is a chance that Boynton Beach might not only experience crowds becoming a lot larger in the summer seasons for obvious reasons. That increased traffic can also lead to more people wanting to buy property in the area, which in turn can increase the demand for real estate.

If more people want real estate, there might be more demand to build houses and that can create a risk of having too much development of properties that could reduce the charm this city has. But that is a risk that can happen in for any of these waterfront property havens. Another concern to consider is the crime index that is slightly above the national average, according to TopRetirements.com.

At the moment, it is still a much quieter city than the nearby metropolitan areas. It offers suburban living with homes that fit various budgets and a population under 100,000. There's no income tax, so you won't need to worry about money coming out of your retirement paycheck. However, expect a sales tax rate of about 6 percent, which by comparison is a lot less than the larger Florida markets like Miami (7 percent), Tampa (7 percent) and Tallahassee (7.5 percent).

If you do decide to move to Boynton Beach and still want to occasionally visit the larger cities as a tourist, Miami is only 50 miles away. Other towns like Delray Beach, Palm Beach and Fort Lauderdale are also just about an hour away by car - which makes for a perfect day trip.

## 3. Fort Meyers, Florida

**Why is it a Great Place to Retire?**

Florida is known for having plenty of beachfront that offers waters coming from the Gulf of Mexico and the Atlantic Ocean. Different parts of the southern half of the state offer an eclectic environment that anyone planning for retirement would put at the top of their wish list. Fort Meyers has a mixture of the old-school design and contemporary architecture. It is home to about 65,000 residents and hundreds of thousands more in neighboring communities that also offer a similar beach environment.

The waterfront home market in Fort Meyers offers a number of properties with a price of more than $1 million for a three bedroom, two-and-a-half bathroom house with almost 5,000 square feet of space. Alternatively, there are smaller properties that are sold for a few hundred thousand dollars with about two or three bedrooms in a 1,200 square feet area. Cap Coral, which is located to the west of Fort Meyers, offers additional waterfront homes and lots for sale for around the same price range.

In addition to single houses for sale, the area also offers a variety of adult living options like senior citizen homes, apartment buildings, and condominiums for rent. Some of these properties do not only offer a close proximity to the Gulf of Mexico, but also offer gated communities and high-rise buildings. A lot of the buildings with vacancies are relatively new as most of them were built in 2006 to provide diverse housing options – different sizes, shapes and prices. Overall, the average price for a home is only about $200,000 after a recent drop in the value of housing.

**Local Community**

Among the things to do in Fort Meyers, one of the most interesting attractions is the Calusa Nature Center and Planetarium – a non-profit private education center that focuses on environmental study built within a 105-acre site. Residents enjoy a very large museum, three different nature trails, a full-size planetarium to study stars and planets, and aviaries with different birds and butterflies. Furthermore, a museum would not be complete without a gift shop and a place to enjoy a nice picnic.

Additionally, Fort Meyers is home to the Imaginarium Science Center – a hands-on science museum and aquarium that provides summer camps for children, which will be a great place for retirees to take their grandchildren.

Fort Meyers also has a historical downtown commercial district that contains nearly 70 different buildings that include the summer homes of inventor, Thomas Edison, and automotive industrialist, Henry Ford, which still stand along McGregor Boulevard near the downtown district – each estate offers tours. In addition to the Edison Estate, there is also the Edison Mall that is a super-sized shopping center with 160 stores in total and more than one million square feet of total retail space.

The historical district also includes the Murphy-Burroughs House located on First Street that officially became an addition to the US National Register of Historic Places in 1984. It was built in 1901 originally with a Georgian Revival style by George Murphy. Eventually, it was sold to Nelson Burroughs in 1918. Similar to the Ford and Edison Estates, the Murphy-Burroughs House offers weekly history tours through the home.

Retirees who love to watch baseball can watch professional-level baseball with the Boston Red Sox of the Major League Baseball. They play at JetBlue Park in Fort Meyers, which is part of the city's Fenway South training and development facility. The Red Sox opened this baseball park in 2012 after spending many years at the City of Palms Park a few miles down the road. This is a popular baseball park that is used by the Red Sox during MLB's Spring Training in March, as well as the Gulf Coast League Red Sox.

In addition to being the spring home for the Red Sox, its American League rival, Minnesota Twins, is also headquartered at Hammond Stadium in Fort Meyers. Hammond Stadium had major renovations in 2014 and 2015 and is now able to host up to 9,300 baseball fans for March's Grapefruit League. Minnesota also has a Gulf Coast League Twins that play rookie-level minor league baseball, similar to the Gulf Coast League Red Sox.

Speaking of sports, there are several options to play a round of golf with several public and private courses – including the El Rio Golf Club, the Fort Myers Country Club, and the Eastwood Golf Course. There are also several places to go fishing in the Gulf of Mexico and do other water activities, like boating, scuba-diving, and surfing. The rest of the downtown area has plenty of charm to go along with the different parks and shopping centers that are world-renowned. But one of the biggest concerns is that Fort Meyers is growing way too fast and having too much development between housing for a growing population and the retail businesses – which can be seen in the extremely large number of strip malls in the area. However, that is expected, especially since Fort Myers' economy is driven by retail and tourism.

In terms of climate, Fort Meyers has what is considered a tropical savannah climate. It offers very short winters that have warmer temperatures than in the northern part of the United States, with the temperatures being up to 75 degrees high. On the other hand, Fort Myers has longer summers that can be very hot and very humid, with temperatures staying closer to around 92 degrees high in July. June is the wettest month of the year with up to 10 inches of rain. Having warmer temperatures can actually be a deal-breaker for some prospective retirees who prefer someplace cooler.

Other communities that offer additional beach opportunities include the neighboring Cape Coral, Bonita Bay, Bonita Springs, Lehigh Acres, and Naples. However, because of the various activities and opportunities found in the communities in Fort Myers, people of various ages and demographics are attracted to it – including a very large school-age population and a growing class of aspiring business owners and professionals.

## 4. Eureka, California

### Why is it a Great Place to Retire?

When someone thinks about the state of California, one would imagine the major cities that sit along the coast of the Pacific Ocean – including San Diego, San Francisco, Long Beach, Malibu, and Santa Monica. But those metropolitan beach cities can be quite expensive to live in due to their popularity – so how can you enjoy the California coast without paying too much?

One of the hidden gems on the West Coast is Eureka, a small port city that rests on California's Humboldt Bay in the northern part of the state – between San Francisco and Portland, Oregon. It was originally a port city that was a key part of the state's logging and commercial fishing businesses since the mid-1800s.

It is also a small town with around 30,000 total residents. The area has amazing views of the bay that opens up into the Pacific Ocean. Amazingly, the prices

36

for homes are very low in this city, according to several listings on Zillow's online real estate listings. Some of the homes that rest near docks of the Humboldt Bay area are priced between $165,000 and $215,000. However, these are rather small with only two bedrooms and a space between 800 to 900 square feet.

But these homes are right next to the water and many of which have their own docks where residents can park their own boats for fishing on their own. There are also some homes that aren't right next to the water but offer amazing views – some of which are a little above $250,000 and $300,000 and offer more living space.

## Local Community

Because Eureka was originally an isolated town that missed a lot of post-war redevelopments seen in other parts of the state after conflicts during the War of 1812, many of the homes and buildings feature 19th and 20$^{th}$ century architecture – which helps make Eureka one of the state's historical landmarks.

Old Town is known for the preserved Victorian era buildings within a commercial district that includes the Richard Sweasey Theater that was first built in 1920 and refurbished in 2007. It currently serves as the home for the Eureka Symphony for a period of time before closing its doors in 2013.

One of the more iconic homes to view is the Milton Carson Home, also known as the "Pink Lady." It is an 1889 Queen Anne Victorian style home that is now a living museum for folks to see. Another iconic home that is a National Historic Landmark in Eureka is the William S. Clarke cottage that was built in 1888. It is known for its Eastlake style of detail for this Victorian home.

There are additional museums and galleries to see for the retiree who enjoys being able to learn about the small city's history – including the Humboldt Bay Maritime Museum, the Morris Graves Museum of Art, and the Blue Ox Millworks and Historic Park. Another option for those with grandchildren is the Discovery Museum for Children.

There has also been an urban renewal in Eureka where there is a growing fine arts community with several groups like the North Coast Repertory Theater, and the Eureka Theater, which help produce several shows throughout the year. In addition to music and dance performances, there are several art organizations that help feature plenty of varieties of visual art, like painting, sculpture, and photography.

There's the Humboldt Arts Council, the Redwood Art Association and then there's the Eureka Art and Culture Commission. The local Humboldt State University is also home to its own First Street Gallery – home to several exhibitions throughout the year for its students and alumni.

The university, which is affiliated with the California State University, is home to about 8,000 students and features different science and arts studies as well as newer energy and environmental programs. The school doesn't have much impact on the retirement lifestyle, so don't worry about running into too many college students around town.

Because Eureka is known as an arts community, it is a big theme for several of the city's annual events. One of the most interesting is the World Championship Kinetic Sculpture Race, which is a contest for creating human-powered works of art that can complete a cross-country style event. It is held during Memorial Day weekend. Eureka also hosts an annual Redwood Coast Jazz Festival in March, the Summer Concert Series on the Boardwalk from June till August, and the Humboldt Bay Full of Blues event in late August.

Another attraction that is a short day-trip from Eureka is the Redwood National and State Parks that are scattered throughout Northern California. It's a great chance to see the massive woodland area with various redwood trees that tower over you. The park also has several trails to walk and drive through, and campsites to make a stop for the night. There are also programs led by California state park rangers who can show more of the redwood forests and other natural attractions throughout California – including the kayak tours of the Klamath River and several nature walks for various state parks.

As far as the weather is concerned, the winters are very mild and will include plenty of rain. The temperatures at this time usually fall between 41 and 60 degrees in December and January. The summers are pretty much like what you expect in California with temperatures as low as 60 degrees and rising up to as much as 80 degrees. One of the things that some prospective retirees may not like is the frequent fog that rolls through Eureka like much of the northern part of the

Pacific coast. Another concern is the crime rate in Eureka, which is a little bit higher than the national average.

However, there are other benefits that make Eureka pretty convenient for the retired residents. The Mud River Community Hospital is just about nine miles away in nearby Arcata. Alternatively, Redwood Memorial Hospital is just about 15 miles away in Fortuna. The nearest airport at Arcata is only 13 miles away from Eureka.

## 5. Rehoboth Beach, Delaware

### Why is it a Great Place to Retire?

Let's say you aren't in the market for an area like Florida or California – states that are often considered the most popular waterfront escape for those looking for their new retirement homes. There are a lot of options that are settled along the Pacific and Atlantic coastlines that offer more than just sunshine and sandy beaches.

One of the most unlikely places that should be on your preliminary list is the state of Delaware – possibly one of the smallest states in the Northeast region behind Rhode Island. But with an area that rests only two hours away from the nation's capital in Washington, DC, Rehoboth Beach, Delaware, is a great option that offers year-round living for both retirees and anyone looking for a relaxing getaway from the extreme hustle and bustle of DC.

It's also located within the pastoral Delmarva Peninsula – which features parts of Delaware, Virginia and Maryland – and is often less noticed by retirement property seekers because there's some extra effort needed to get to this beach oasis. That means there is likely to be less tourist traffic than some of the other Atlantic Coast communities found in places like Florida, Virginia and the Carolinas.

43

The main Coastal Highway doesn't enter Rehoboth Beach and actually goes around the town. Main roads, for the most part, very rarely go through the city. When it comes to transportation around the city, the options include what is commonly called by locals as "beach buses" – providing service in and around the various Delaware beaches and other state parks.

Housing can be quite pricey, but not as high as the multi-million homes in California and Florida. According to TopRetirements.com, the median price for a home in Rehoboth Beach is a little more than $400,000 as of last year – much more expensive than retirement hot-beds nearby, like Georgetown and other inland communities.

## Local Community

What makes this Delaware beach community a good choice is the lack of sales tax, as well as paying lower property taxes. This will come in consideration when you think about the being able to purchase from the

Rehoboth Beach Farmer's Market, or go dining at one of the well-known restaurants like Nicolas Restaurant – the home of the popular Nic-o-boli, a whole pizza that is wrapped into a calzone.

Speaking of good food, the Apple Dumplings Etc is known for a donut breakfast sandwich. You might also want to get your fix of fresh seafood and sushi at Cultured Pearl.

One of the biggest attractions of Rehoboth Beach is the mile-long boardwalk that runs parallel to the beaches that welcome the waters of the Atlantic Ocean. This boardwalk features several retail options that include several local shops that are unique to the rest of the country. There are also additional outlet stores that can provide a really good bargain.

The Rehoboth Beach boardwalk features a variety of activities to enjoy, including the Dogfish Head Brewery tour, as well as a day trip option to the city's lavender farm and Jungle Jim's Waterpark – perfect for visiting grandchildren.

One of the other things that Rehoboth Beach prides itself is the calendar of annual festivals that reach various demographics, including the Autumn Rehoboth Jazz Festival in October for the eclectic music enthusiast, the Chocolate Festival in March for the foodie, and the Seawitch Festival in October that features a big sandcastle contest where adults can unleash their creative inner-child at the beach.

In addition to being able to have fun at various annual festivals, there are plenty of ways to enjoy the outdoors, like swimming in the nearby beach, boating, skiing and other water sports. There are also 12 public golf courses where you could have a private instructor for an additional fee per round of golf. There are also plenty of fishing grounds within the proximity of Rehoboth Beach.

With regards to entertainment, there are several productions from the Henlopen Theater Project, the Rehoboth Summer Children's Theater, and other theater groups. Likewise, there are different concerts at the city's bandstand. There is also a Rehoboth Art League to promote the fine arts and an annual Rehoboth Film Festival.

Other attractions include the Rehoboth Beach Historical Society, Overfalls Maritime Museum, the Anna Hazard Museum, and several more movie theaters and museums.

Because of the large increase in senior citizens coming to the area for retirement, the average age of Rehoboth Beach residents has increased to about 59 years old. This means there will be plenty of elder-friendly perks throughout the homes and the city – like having beaches that are accessible by wheelchair. There are also a mixed diversity of families, seniors, and even gay and lesbian couples enjoying the tranquility of the

Atlantic Ocean – some of whom actually live in Rehoboth Beach seasonally.

The weather is very moderate in comparison to the rest of the Atlantic Coastal Plain with hot and humid summers and mild winters. At the hottest peak temperature in July, the average daytime high is 87 degrees and the lowest is about 70. On the flip side, January highs average in the upper 40-degree mark and the lowest point hovers around 30 degrees – just a tiny bit below freezing. There is also rain, with the most coming in July at about four to five inches, while February has the least with just above three inches on an average throughout the month.

## 6. Port Townsend, Washington

### Why is it a Great Place to Retire?

When most people start looking towards the Pacific Northwest, many people tend to think about Seattle, which is nicknamed the "Emerald City" that sits on the

Puget Sound – complete with views of the water and Mount Rainier in the distance. However, there are plenty more cities and towns that offer the same type of views without the extremely expensive price tags that are attached to waterfront properties – which makes a town like Port Townsend one of the most economical choices for those planning to live near the water when they retire.

Located in a small town across the Puget Sound to the northeast of Seattle, there is the small town of Port Townsend. It is considered by many to be a town lost in time with neighborhoods filled with Victorian buildings that have aged well over time within the town's designated national historical district.

The historical area includes the Fort Worden State Park, which once served as an Army base that was first established in the early 1900s to help create a strategic defense of the Puget Sound region. Many of the Army's finest were stationed here leading up to World

War I before much of it was moved to Europe – leaving behind one of the town's best tourist attractions and US military landmarks.

The state park is also home for an annual camp for children offered by the Jefferson County Historical Society – which provides an opportunity for learning and fun for visiting grandchildren that might come during the summer months or other holidays throughout the year.

## Local Community

The downtown corridor of Port Townsend features several coffee houses, cafes, and businesses that offer niche items and antiques, which is why it shouldn't be of any surprise that the town features a very busy arts and crafts demographic that produce a list of popular festivals. One of the biggest events of the year is the Victorian Spring Ball where the town's early history of being a seaport is celebrated.

Additionally, the town's Fort Worden State Park is also known for the thriving arts center – the Centrum – which is home to several more festivals, including the annual film festival. The Centrum also hosts monthly Gallery Walks held on the first Saturday of each month as well as regular productions through the Key City Public Theater.

While the town is small, there is no shortage of a talented fine arts community, which includes more than theater enthusiasts and musicians. There are authors, song writers, dancers, and visual artists with a wide range of experience in their respective fields – from 16-year-olds honing their painting skills to those in their 80s who are still actively writing their own music.

One of the biggest music festivals in the Pacific Northwest region is the Jazz Port Townsend – the longest-running jazz festival that usually takes place every July. It features an opportunity to experience several different musicians in the setting of downtown Port Townsend. Many of the performances are done in local nightclubs, theaters, and in outdoor parks.

According to TopRetirements.com, Port Townsend has a very small population of just above 9,100. It has a median home cost of about $267,000 with property taxes costing closer to $2,000 each year – which is a smaller amount compared to many other waterfront cities that will be mentioned later on. The site does support the numbers of how many homes were built multiple decades ago.

For example, about 17 percent of the homes in Port Townsend were built before the 1940s. At the same time, a little more than 20 percent of homes were built between 2000 and 2009 – which shows a blend of modern and classic home architecture to provide for the various tastes of prospective buyers.

Many of the homes are built from brick and offer amazing views of nearby Mount Rainier and the Puget Sound. It is also very secluded with many commuters needing to take a ferry boat across the Puget Sound to access this part of the Olympic Peninsula. A ferry ride from Port Townsend to Seattle usually takes about an hour and a half, which means it doesn't take too much of an effort to make a day trip to Pike Place Market, or catch a Seattle Mariners baseball game at Safeco Field.

Without the ferry, you would have to take a long drive that would act as a tour of the rest of the Olympic Peninsula to the south with other quaint little towns like Bremerton and Shelton before going back north towards Olympia, Tacoma and into Seattle. There are several state parks that feature different camping grounds and varying views of the multiple mountains, canals, rivers and forests throughout the state. In fact, there is more to see by making a car trip that only lasts a few hours to see different towns located along the coast near the Pacific Ocean.

Being close to a lot of parks also provides countless offerings for various outdoors activities – mountain climbing, fishing, kayaking, trail hiking, and hunting to name a few. When the snow begins to fall during the winter months, there are several skiing opportunities at locations that can be reached within a day's drive – including Crystal Mountain, Stevens Pass, and the Summit at Snoqualmie.

Because of the distance the town has from Washington's larger metropolitan areas, there is a much lower crime rate compared to the US average. This means that those who wish to live in a safe and secluded neighborhood with great views will possibly find their perfect place in Port Townsend.

Because Port Townsend is located within the Pacific Northwest, prospective retirees should consider that there will be a higher chance of rain for more than half of the year and only a few sunbreaks between the fall and winter months. But all of that rain eventually leads to a budding spring and beautiful summers that allow residents and regional tourists to see Mother Nature's beauty.

## 7. Bandon, Oregon

### Why is it a Great Place to Retire?

When thinking about the advantages of living in the Pacific Northwest, a major factor that is considered by retirees to make the move is the ability to live in the middle of a beautiful oasis of nature that is far away from any large city, or even mid-major markets that include a large number of people, traffic, and crime. Brandon, Oregon, is one of those towns that provide an escape from the busy cities and a chance to live in an area near the ocean that also includes forests, trails, and other outdoor activities like hiking, windsurfing, fishing, and golf.

Bandon is a small town – remotely located in the mountainous area of the Pacific Northwest – which is growing, but still remains well below the mark of 5,000 residents. It is surrounded by high cliffs above the Pacific Ocean that wash onto large beachfronts. These cliffs also provide amazing rock formations that are home to multiple types of sea creatures that are amazing to see up-close. This is one of the reasons why Bandon is one of the Pacific Northwest's top tourist towns.

When it comes to living along the coast of Bandon, homes can be very expensive the closer you are to the water – but those higher price tags come with a great value in return. For example, $850,000 can purchase a beautiful wood constructed three-bedroom house with two bathrooms and nearly 2,000 square feet of living space.

A beachfront home about a mile north with a beautiful view of Pacific Ocean and a beachfront instead of a typical suburban backyard goes for just a little more than $1.1 million. The average listing price for a home in Brandon, Oregon, is just under $400,000 – a very low price when looking at some of the other price listings for cities farther down south along the Pacific Coast.

**Local Community**

When it comes to retirees wanting to pursue or maintain an active lifestyle, Bandon provides a very diverse community that includes world class golf, a setting near the Pacific Ocean, and charm found in an average small town. With everything considered, there is no excuse for not finding something to do for fun and entertainment.

Bandon has four of the country's best courses, including the Bandon Dunes Golf Resort and Pacific Dunes Course that both run down the Pacific coast. Additionally, the Old McDonald Golf Course, and Bandon Trails provide unique experiences of being able to walk within nature while still being able to look at amazing views of the Pacific Ocean.

Bandon has a lot of qualities that are very similar to Ireland beyond the love of golf. The terrain of the city's golf courses is identical to Ireland's western coast, with everything from the hillsides and the course – which can also be seen in Irish golf courses like Tralee Golf Club, and Ballybunion Golf Club.

This Oregon town goes well beyond golf for its offering to the outdoor enthusiast. Bandon is also known for the various opportunities for fishing within the Pacific Ocean as well as various parks and nature trails to get lost in – a perfect way to escape the busy city life.

One of the most unique activities that are frequented in Bandon is coastal storm watching, with skies becoming gray and the winds crashing the waves of the Pacific Ocean into the beaches and rock formations. The best time of the year to enjoy watching the storms of the Pacific Northwest is during the winter months of January and February.

Bandon also provides various opportunities to enjoy the arts, including the Bandon Playhouse and the Bandon Showcase that produce various plays and cultural events. There are also several community events that include the Bandon Chamber of Commerce's annual Cranberry Festival which has been celebrated for almost 70 years. This is because Brandon is known for its cranberry production, which is about 95 percent of the state's cranberry supply.

But the one thing that the town of Bandon celebrates the most is nature. A local non-profit organization called the Shoreline Education for Awareness (SEA Inc.) creates educational programs about the Pacific Coast shoreline and teaches people about the different wildlife that makes the beaches and rock formations a natural habitat.

Speaking of natural habitats, Bandon is also home to the West Coast Game Park Safari that opened in 1968 and has been home to several wild animals like snow leopards, Bengal tigers, lions, black bears, cougars, emu, and capybara – the largest species of rodent on Earth. With the park operating as a petting zoo to the public with a captive breeding program, these animals are oftentimes raised to be eventually sold to other parks and wildlife zoos across the country.

Bandon is also the home of the Bullards Beach State Park, which is highlighted by the Coquille River Lighthouse that stands off the coast in the middle of the Pacific Ocean. The lighthouse was originally built in 1895 and was given major restorations in the 1970s, after 37 years of being deactivated. Now, it is one of the most iconic tourist attractions in Oregon. There is also a new solar powered lighthouse that was given in 1991 with a range of about 14 miles.

There are also additional side notes about the little town of Bandon, including the fact that dairy and cheese production was once a big part of the local economy between the 1920s until 2000. Since then, the Brandon Cheese Company was rebranded as Tillamook Cheese by the Tillamook County Creamery Association – which is very famous in the Pacific Northwest for cheese, ice cream and frozen yogurt at various grocery stores in Oregon, Idaho, Washington and northern California.

With regards to the climate in Bandon, the average high temperature reaches 67 degrees in the summer months and can fall to as low as 38 degrees in the winter in January. While it rains only a little in those summer months, it usually falls in December at an average of 10 inches of rainfall per year.

## 8. Williamsburg, Virginia

### Why is it a Great Place to Retire?

The state of Virginia has become the home of people who came from the northern states in the US as it offers a lot of premiere places for retirement – such as Alexandria, Prince George, and Williamsburg.

Although it has a mid-sized college with thousands of students, and history enthusiasts converge in Williamsburg for the sites of the American Revolution, it is still one of the more attractive retirement destinations in the country.

Williamsburg has one of the lowest crime rates across the country. It is one of the original colonial cities and is located near the easternmost part of the state along the Atlantic Coast. This coastal city is included in the top five lists of *Best Places to Live* by Money Magazine due to several factors, including cost of living, things to do, and spectacular views of the Atlantic Ocean. All of these factors make

Williamsburg one of the most desirable places to live for senior citizens above the age of 55 who prefer a less hectic lifestyle setting. With a little more than 12,000 residents and around 40,000 visiting tourists every year, Williamsburg is a good fit for that preference. However, if you want to have an exciting day trip, there are plenty of busy cities to visit nearby. Norfolk, Virginia, for one, is only about 40 miles away.

Although this part of Virginia has a cost of living that is a little bit higher than the average American city, people still choose to live in Williamsburg for the big reason that it offers a variety for all forms of family. While some of the homes closer to the mainland of Virginia can range between $150,000 and $300,000, many of the waterfront properties can range a little bit higher – depending on the amenities, rooms, and amount of living space.

For example, Zillow shows a four bedroom home with three and a half bathrooms and 4,100 square feet will cost about $1.8 million. A little further to the west along the beaches of James River is a 1,300-square foot home with two bedrooms and two bathrooms for $299,000 – not a bad deal for a retired couple that doesn't need too much space.

What makes Williamsburg unique is that the home prices have remained at the same rate for the past few years, which has also allowed the property taxes to be lower than the national average. The prices are considered high because of how it has gained so much popularity – a little bit like everyone hearing about the well-kept secret beach that is leaked and all of a sudden filled with surfers.

Many of the homes in Williamsburg are antique homes in the downtown area, as well as near the ocean beaches – similar to what you see in an 18th century museum. At the same time, there are also plenty of recently developed homes and apartment buildings built in a more upscale manner.

**Local Community**

With its history dating back to 1632 as one of the first commonwealths that later became the United States of America, Williamsburg attracts tourists who wish to see the Colonial Williamsburg neighborhood – a site of some of the most important dates during the American Revolution in the late 1700s. The city's culture revolves around the colonial background and history enthusiasts enjoy the place as they find something historical around every corner.

For the retiree who loves to study and learn, the Williamsburg Regional Library can keep you busy with more than 281,000 volumes to read through. There are also plenty of courses for all ages that want to continue learning through the Christopher Wren Association – sponsored by the College of William and Mary and teach nearly 2,000 students.

Speaking of William and Mary, the school has a long history that dates back to its creation in 1693 and attracts more than 8,000 total undergraduate and graduate students. The college also plays Division I athletics in the Colonial Athletic Association – so there's a chance to watch some college basketball as the Tribe plays teams like James Madison University, Elon University, Drexel University, and Hofstra University (schools who have played in past NCAA men's basketball tournaments as upset-minded teams).

At the same time, there are a lot of notable locations mixed in to add some depth beyond that 18th century feel of the town. Anheuser-Busch – known best for making several brands of beer, including Budweiser and Bud Light – operates a very large brewery in Williamsburg as well as two theme parks nearby.

The first is Busch Gardens, a theme park with nearly 400 acres with more than 50 different amusement park rides – including seven roller coasters and three water rides. The second park is Water Country USA, which is the largest water park in the Mid-Atlantic. It is owned by SeaWorld Entertainment with 17 total rides that are available between May and September.

With regards to the town's climate and environment, the city is mostly flat with plenty of waterways. In addition to the nearby Atlantic Ocean, Williamsburg is part of the Virginia Peninsula that is bounded by Chesapeake Bay, James River, and York River. The summers can be pretty warm with the average high during the month of July around 89 degrees. It is also at this time when most of the rain falls. On the flip side, Virginia can get pretty cold and Williamsburg has seen the average low in January to about 28 degrees. Williamsburg provides a very balanced mix of weather for those who prefer experiencing all four seasons that aren't always available in some waterfront locations like Florida and California.

There are several additional factors that have led to the growing number of interested retirees. These include having two different medical facilities to go to in case of emergencies or other health care services. The first one is a newer, 145-bed facility of the Sentara Williamsburg Regional Medical Center – which is in addition to the Eastern State Hospital. Both nearby cities, Richmond and Hampton, have more options, including the Veterans Administration hospital.

For those who have families visiting from out of state, the Newport News/Williamsburg Airport is only about 25 minutes away from the small town. There are also additional options that are just within an hour's drive – the Norfolk International Airport and Richmond International Airport.

## 9. Traverse City, Michigan

### Why is it a Great Place to Retire?

While the summer sun and sandy beaches in areas like southern California and Florida are popular among retirees, there are those who have grown up in the Midwestern region and wouldn't want to stray too far away from the place they've known for most of their lives.

In this case, a great alternative would be to find a city along one of the lake-states like Michigan, Illinois or Minnesota. One of the more popular retirement locations like this is Traverse City, Michigan, which provides miles of beaches along Lake Michigan with waterfront living options for much less than the options farther south or on the West Coast.

Living in Traverse City is considered pretty inexpensive when compared to the national average. Some homes cost less than $300,000 for a four bedroom home that offers more than 2,000 square feet of living space. There are also several lots where you can build a home along the water for prices that fall below the $200,000 mark.

Even with more than 125,000 residents living in Traverse City, there is still a small town feel unlike in the Midwest's largest metropolitan cities like Chicago and Detroit. Moreover, Traverse City has a much lower crime rate than those larger cities.

## Local Community

Because Traverse City rests close to Lake Michigan, there are several outdoor activities that you could do when the weather cooperates. For example, many folks enjoy the par-72 Elmbrook Golf Course that has a five-star rating from various online sources. The same is true with the Bay Meadows Golf Course that features a lot of the surrounding nature to provide a tranquil golfing experience.

There are also several boating options during the spring and summer months. Likewise, there are plenty of beaches to enjoy like the Sleeping Bear Dunes National Lakeshore – a 35-mile long park which includes a number of forests, beaches, dunes, and ancient glaciers that have been formed over long periods of time. Since 1970, the park has grown with several offerings to enjoy – the Sleeping Bear Point Coast Guard Station, Maritime Museum, Glen Haven Village, and Port Oneida Historic Farm District.

The Traverse City State Park is rather large with about 250 camping sites within 50 acres of land that also includes a quarter-mile beachfront along the eastern part of the Grand Traverse Bay. So there are plenty of outdoor options for those who want to bring a large tent or maybe a recreational vehicle (RV) and enjoy having nature surround you for the evening.

There's also a series of road bicycling trails using the "TART trail system" that offers several routes to traverse while also providing advice and tips on each course you take. There are also several opportunities to go sailing, kayaking, or fishing on Lake Michigan.

However, these outdoor activities are often forgotten when the very cold winter arrives, which often brings plenty of snow. During this time, however, there are several ski resort options for activities, such as skiing and snowboarding at the Hickory Hills Ski Area, which features eight different runs with varying difficulties for each.

In the summer months, Traverse City averages just above 80 degrees in July with a corresponding low of 58 degrees. But when it cools down, it really gets low with the highest temperatures in January reaching just a tad below 30 degrees and down to about 15 degrees during the evening. But for the most part, temperatures very rarely reach triple digits and there won't be many days below 0 degrees – although it has happened in the past.

Beyond the outdoor activities, Traverse City is considered one of the most active arts communities in the United States. Part of that is due to the Interlochen Center, which hosts more than 700 different events throughout the year that include concerts, art exhibits, and different productions of theater and dance. Additionally, there are more fine arts venues like the Music House Museum, the Old Town Playhouse, the Encore Society of Music, the Traverse Symphony Orchestra, and the Dennos Museum, which is located within Northwestern Michigan College.

And what goes well with the fine arts but fine wine. Traverse City has plenty of options as it is within the Old Mission Peninsula wine region – a 19,200 acre lot that grows several types of grapes for different wines – Chardonnay, Malbec, Gewurztraminer, and Cabernet Sauvignon. The region is also home to nine wineries many of which will offer free tastings to the general public.

Retirees can also enjoy the annual National Cherry Festival often held in July in Traverse City. During this time, you have the opportunity to watch the cherry blossoms begin to bloom for the summer season – an event that often attracts more than 500,000 people every year.

For the sports fan, there are plenty of teams to get interested in like the Traverse City Beach Bums in minor league baseball's Frontier League, the Traverse City Cohos junior-level hockey league squad, and a semi-professional football team called the Traverse City Wolves of the North American Football League. The city also hosts training camp for the Detroit Red Wings before the start of the National Hockey League season. Traverse City also hosts the Traverse City Prospects Tournament for young NL prospects playing for select NHL teams.

Another consideration for retirees is Munson Medical Center that has highly positive ratings and is a regional medical center serving patients from more than 30 Michigan counties. There's also the Cherry Capitol Airport that connects with Chicago, Detroit and Minneapolis regularly. The Bay Area Transportation Agency also offers bus services.

An object of concern for some retirees may be the tourists who usually come for the National Cherry Festival – half a million in total. However, tourism is a big part of the local economy, much like the other cities and communities discussed earlier.

## 10. Dubuque, Iowa

**Why is it a Great Place to Retire?**

The previous cities mentioned in this list have focused on being next to oceans, bays, lakes and canals. But what about living down by the river? One of the most cost-sensitive ideas is in the Midwest. Dubuque, Iowa, offers plenty of low-cost housing options that have either amazing views of the river, or are right next to it.

According to Zillow, some of the smaller homes are currently listed for less than $100,000. These types of homes usually include three bedrooms with 1,400 square feet of living space that sit along the Mississippi River. Alternatively, other homes that offer just two bedrooms and less than 900 square feet of living space are listed for less than $80,000.

That doesn't mean that there are not more expensive homes. It is just that they just aren't as rampant as in some of the other cities like California, Florida, and South Carolina. In fact, one home currently listed for $400,000 offers five bedrooms, four bathrooms, and about 4,500 square feet of living space. Overall, the average home is a little under the $200,000 price tag.

What makes Dubuque unique is that the city is at a junction of Iowa, Illinois and Wisconsin as part of a

Tri-State area that is sometimes called the "City of Five Flags." Its population is less than 60,000 residents, but that number is expected to change as Dubuque is starting to gain some popularity among retirees who are not only coming from those three Midwestern states, but also want something different from the usual sandy beaches, and are looking for a more quiet setting.

**Local Community**

Dubuque also attracts a lot of tourists because of the several highlights within the downtown corridor, starting with the National Mississippi River Museum and Aquarium – which might be a good place to take the visiting grandchildren for some fun education. At the same time, there are also a lot of gaming opportunities for those who like to play some blackjack or slot machines. There's the Diamond Jo Casino and the Mystique Casino. Likewise, there are

77

also several riverboat casinos located throughout Iowa, including Dubuque.

Fine art opportunities abound in this Iowa town, which includes the Dubuque Symphony Orchestra – a non-union professional orchestra that casts 75 musicians that perform classical, chamber, opera, and pop music. They have about 25 shows every year in 12 different counties of Iowa, Illinois, and Wisconsin.

Dubuque is also home for the Colts Drum and Bugle Corps, which is a top-notch ensemble that tours the country every summer for multiple drum corps competitions against other nationalities. One of their annual highlights is hosting a "Music on the March" competition that is an internationally-sanctioned marching competition held at Dubuque Senior High School.

Dubuque's Grand Opera House, which is currently celebrating its 125th anniversary, is also one of those live performance venues that conduct special lecture events hosted by nationally recognized figures. Other downtown attractions include the Dubuque Shot Tower, the Five Flags Civic Center, and the Gran River Center.

Dubuque also has several buildings that are on the National Register of Historic Places that some retirees enjoy visiting. For example, the Dubuque Arboretum and Botanical Gardens have won several awards, including being considered one of the largest hosta gardens that is open to the public with about 13,000 different plants with more than 700 different types represented.

Other national landmarks include the Dubuque County Courthouse – partly due to the unique Beaux-Arts design, the Julien Dubuque Bridge, and the Linwood Cemetery -- which is home to several notable people. There is also the Ice Harbor waterfront to the north end of the city that features several buildings currently being refurbished for a new business complex to go along with the Diamond Jo Casino and the Grand River Event Center.

For the sports fan, there might not be any big name teams from the National Football League, National Basketball Association, or Major League Baseball. However, Dubuque has a history of developmental hockey, starting from being the initial home of the Fighting Saints junior-level team in the United States Hockey League from 1980 to 2001 before the team was moved to Tulsa, Oklahoma. The Dubuque Thunderbirds would fill the void while playing in the Central States Hockey League and even won the USHL Clark Cup championship by defeating the Green Bay Gamblers in a three-game sweep in 2011.

The city has grown in recent years, being listed as the 22nd highest growth back in 2005 – standing out amongst the rest of the state of Iowa with more than 10 percent increase in new jobs. A big reason for this is the jobs created by companies like the John Deere Company, Sedgwick CMS, and Quebecor World Inc.

Like other retirement hotbeds, Dubuque has plenty of health-care options that are a big deciding factor for several retirees. In fact, it is one of the largest in the Tri-State region that covers eastern Iowa, Northwestern Illinois, and Southwestern Wisconsin. One of the big medical hospitals in Dubuque is the Mercy Medical Center, which offers 263 beds. It is one of only three hospitals in the state to achieve the "Magnet Hospital" status – one that meets strict standards as one of the best facilities in the US.

The second hospital in Dubuque is the Finley Hospital – a member of the UnityPoint Health network – with about 148 hospitals and is considered a top choice for those who are diagnosed with cancer because of the top-rated oncology facilities within the complex. Additional health care facilities include the Medical Associates Clinic that have east and west campuses and offers more outpatient clinics, internal medicine, and other specialists.

All these factors are the reason why Dubuque is gaining the interest of more retirees. Thus being said, if you are planning to retire in the very near future, you might want to start looking into when you will be able to start making a property purchase to ensure that you get a good spot near the river – before the development puts the quiet town at risk of not having enough room for everyone who is interested.

# Conclusion

After reading this list, you might have discovered that having a waterfront property is more than just living near the ocean or a very large lake. There are riverfronts that are a little bit cheaper than other options that can be found in the more central states like Iowa and Illinois. Then there are other locations along those coastal states that offer more financial benefits beyond the lower housing costs.

You may want to live in a home next to the Pacific Ocean along the southern California coastline, but you also don't want to spend several hundred thousands of dollars, or even a couple of million dollars. A better option would be either the northern part of the state in a city like Eureka, or farther up North towards Oregon and Washington – properties that also offer more state parks, forests, mountain trails, and golf courses with more colorful greens and fairways.

The property you would want to purchase also depends on what you want to do, especially if you are the type of person who enjoys the outdoor lifestyle. Camping is better in less congested states like Virginia, Washington, and Iowa – which are much farther from the bigger cities and provide a better chance of getting away from the hustle and bustle stressors of city life. However, if you are the type who prefers to do a variety of water sports like water skiing and surfing, the coastal states of California and Florida might be the best options for you.

One of the important things to consider is being able to find plenty of activities and entertainment options for not only the senior citizens, but also for your grandchildren who might come to visit during the summer breaks. That's why some prospective retirees consider how many water parks, zoos, aquariums, and other destinations are near them – even if it requires a short day drive.

At the same time, you can always look for educational options that provide fun activities where the grandchildren can also learn something – such as fine arts and hands-on museums.

In conclusion, one of the biggest factors to consider is your retirement portfolio and how much money you have saved to purchase a property. While your savings might be enough to purchase one of those larger homes on the beach with 5,000 square feet and seven bedrooms, you also have to consider the fact that this fund shall replace your active income since you will be putting an end to the 9AM-5PM daily grind. Careful planning is necessary to plan for your new home and your daily expenses (food, utilities and transportation), especially if you weren't working in one of the most lucrative careers.

# Final Word/About the Author

Usually I write works around sports to learn more about influential athletes in the hopes that from my writing, you the reader can walk away inspired to put in an equal if not greater amount of hard work and perseverance to pursue your goals. However, I decided to write a few books on retirement to share my own experiences in finding affordable places to retire, as well as adopting newer-age retirement philosophies. I enjoy learning about the different cultures and lifestyles of different towns and sharing them with people beginning to explore their retirement options. If you enjoyed *Best Places to Retire: The Top 10 Most Affordable Waterfront Places for Retirement* please leave a review! Also, you can read more of my general works on *Best Places to Retire: The Top 15 Affordable Towns for Retirement in Asia, Best Places to Retire: The Top 15 Affordable Towns for Retirement in Europe, Best Places to Retire: The Top 15 Affordable*

*Towns for Retirement in Florida, Best Places to Retire: The Top 15 Affordable Towns for Retirement on a Budget, How to Fundraise, How to Get out of the Friend Zone, Narcissistic Personality Disorder, Avoidant Personality Disorder, Sundown Syndrome, ISTJs, ISFJs, ISFPs, INTJs, INFPs, INFJs, ESFPs, ESFJs, ESTJs, ENFPs, ENFJs, ENTJs, How to be Witty, How to be Likeable, How to be Creative, Bargain Shopping, Productivity Hacks, Morning Meditation, Becoming a Father,* and *33 Life Lessons: Success Principles, Career Advice & Habits of Successful People* in the Kindle Store.

# Like what you read?

I write because I love sharing personal development information on topics like retirement with fantastic readers like you. My readers inspire me to write more so please do not hesitate to let me know what you thought by leaving a review! If you love books on life, basketball, or productivity, check out my website at claytongeoffreys.com to join my exclusive list where I let you know about my latest books. Aside from being the first to hear about my latest releases, you can also download a free copy of _33 Life Lessons: Success Principles, Career Advice & Habits of Successful People_. See you there!

33 LIFE LESSONS

SUCCESS PRINCIPLES, CAREER ADVICE
& HABITS OF SUCCESSFUL PEOPLE

CLAYTON GEOFFREYS

# References

1. Multiple listings. www.zillow.com. Web.

2. Multiple articles. www.zillow.com. Web.

3. Petrie, Shannon. "How to Choose a Waterfront Property." *HGTV*. N.p., n.d. Web.

4. Glink, Ilyce. "Top 10 Beach Towns for Retirees." *CBSNews*. CBS Interactive. 10 May 2014. Web.

Made in the USA
San Bernardino, CA
12 December 2017